P9-CCP-973

BUILDING

AMERICA

The Sears Tower

Craig A. Doherty and Katherine M. Doherty

A BLACKBIRCH PRESS BOOK

WOODBRIDGE, CONNECTICUT

Special Thanks

The authors wish to thank the many librarians who helped them find the research materials for this series—especially Donna Campbell, Barbara Barbieri, Yvonne Thomas, and the librarians at the New Hampshire State Library.

The publisher would like to thank Karla Kaulfuss, of Skidmore, Owings & Merrill; Perry D. Chlan, of Sears Roebuck and Co.; Karen Tilling, of Morse Diesel Construction Co.; Dinah Reed, of The John Buck Company; Linda Ziemer of the Chicago Historical Society; and Sandy Spikes, of The Chicago Tribune for their valuable help in putting this book together.

Many thanks to Susan Mastro and the Chicago Architecture Foundation; McShane Fleming Studios; and Mr. Melvyn Skvarla, who were a great help in illustrating this book.

Published by Blackbirch Press, Inc.
One Bradley Road
Woodbridge, CT 06525

© 1995 Blackbirch Press, Inc.
First Edition

Printed in Hong Kong

10 9 8 7 6 5 4 3 2 1

Photo Credits

Cover: ©Steve Vidler/Leo de Wys, Inc.
Title page: ©Peter Pearson/Leo de Wys, Inc.; Pages 4, 8, 32: courtesy Sears Roebuck & Co.; page 6: ©Steve Vidler/Leo de Wys, Inc.; pages 11, 12, 13, 16: courtesy Skidmore, Owings, & Merrill; pages 18, 23: Chicago Tribune; page 20: Chicago Historical Society; pages 21, 23, 24: McShane Fleming Studios/courtesy Chicago Architecture Foundation; page 28: Harr, Hedrich-Blessing; pages 30–31: Bill Engdahl, Hedrich-Blessing; page 32: Harr, Hedrich-Blessing; page 35: ©Hedrich-Blessing/courtesy John Buck Co.; page 37: ©Peter Pearson/Leo de Wys, Inc.; page 39: ©Bruce Glassman; page 41: ©Peter Pearson/Leo de Wys, Inc.; pages 42-43: ©Steve Vidler/Leo de Wys, Inc.

Library of Congress Cataloging-in-Publication Data

Doherty, Katherine M.
   The Sears Tower / by Katherine M. Doherty and Craig A. Doherty.—1st ed.
        p. cm.—(Building America)
   Includes bibliographical references (p.) and index.
   ISBN 1-56711-109-2 (lib. bdg. : alk. paper)
   1. Sears Tower (Chicago, Ill.)—Juvenile literature. 2. Skyscrapers—Illinois—Chicago—Design and construction—Juvenile literature. 3. Chicago (Ill.)—Buildings, structures, etc.—Juvenile literature. [1. Sears Tower (Chicago, Ill.) 2. Skyscrapers—Design and construction.] I. Doherty, Craig A. II. Title. III. Series: Building America (Woodbridge, Conn.)
NA6233.C4S433 1995   94-40642
725'.230483'0977311—dc20   CIP
                                                                     AC

Table of Contents

Introduction

In 1886, Richard Warren Sears started selling gold-filled pocket watches as a sideline to his job with the railroad in North Redwood, Minnesota. At the time, no one imagined that his fledgling R. W. Watch Company would become the largest retailer in the world. By the late 1960s, when the idea of building the Sears Tower was first suggested, Sears Roebuck and Company had annual sales of almost $8.9 billion and a net income of almost $450 million a year. Sears had 355,000 employees working at 826 retail stores, 11 catalog plants, and 2,100 sales offices and

The sleek, black figure of the Sears Tower dominates Chicago's downtown skyline.

independent catalog stores. It also did business in 13 other countries around the world. At the time, Sears generated one percent of the gross national product (the value of all the goods and services produced in a country in a year) of the United States.

To many people in the company in the late 1960s, it seemed only natural that the world's largest retailer should have the world's tallest building. The plan was to erect a building that would eventually provide work space for more than 13,000 of the Sears employees in the Chicago area.

As built, the Sears Tower is the tallest building in the world at 1,454 feet. Its 110 floors combine to provide 4.5 million square feet of space. At the time it was completed in 1973, only the Pentagon—the headquarters of the U.S. military—had more floor space.

The Sears Tower floor space, if laid out on one level, would cover 101 acres, or the equivalent of 16 city blocks in Chicago. Within the building, there are 25 miles of plumbing, 1,500 miles of electric wiring, 80 miles of elevator cable, and 145,000 light fixtures. The building weighs more than 222,500 tons, and it cost more than $160 million to build. It was reported that $12 million of that went to buying the three-acre site in downtown Chicago.

The reasoning behind creating such a large building had to do with Sears's projected growth figures into the 21st century. In the late 1960s, computer-generated analyses of Sears—based on the company's historical growth and an optimistic view of the future—made it look as though the company would need a very large building in the near future. None of the people or the computers in the organization, however, foresaw a slowdown in the economy. Neither did they predict the tremendous success of such discount retailers as Wal-Mart and Kmart during the time the Tower was being planned and built.

Defining the Needs

After they had decided to build a new corporate headquarters, the executives at Sears had to decide where they wanted to locate it. Some thought the suburbs would be best, while others thought that Sears should stay in Chicago. Careful studies were done to decide which location would be most suitable. The company's executives finally learned that staying in the city would create the least amount of disruption for company employees. Many employees depended on public transportation to get to their current offices, which were scattered about the city. Moving out of town would mean losing a lot of those employees. Sears executives finally decided to find a

Opposite:
The Sears Tower stands on a three-acre site in the heart of downtown Chicago.

9

site in the city that would be accessible by public transportation.

Private developers had already started putting together what would become the site for the Sears Tower. Hundreds of tenants lost their leases in the 15 old, run-down buildings that made up the two blocks that would eventually become the location for the Tower. A deal also had to be made with the city to buy the section of Quincy Street that separated the two blocks. Sears ended up paying the city of Chicago $2.7 million for that section of town. With all their real estate deals completed by February 1969, Sears had the three-acre site it needed for its new home.

Finding the Right Architect

Sears's first step in building the Tower was to hire Cushman and Wakefield, one of the country's top real estate development companies, to assist in the promotion and marketing of the Tower. Sears's plan, originally, had been to build a large structure and to rent out about half of it, while its corporate staff grew into the new building.

Cushman and Wakefield was also given the task of selecting the architects to design the building, and it interviewed nine different firms. Its final rec-ommendation was to hire the Chicago office of Skidmore, Owings, and Merrill (SOM). At SOM, Bruce Graham was the partner who was put in charge of designing the project. Noted engineer Fazlur Khan was asked to be the chief structural engineer.

Sears also hired Saphier, Lerner, and Schindler, a company expert in planning space utilization, to plan the inside of the building. These plans would be based on interviews with the top management at Sears, as well as on computer-generated reports on the expected growth of Sears.

By the 1970s, Graham and Khan were one of the nation's most experienced teams when it came to designing tall buildings. They had completed the John Hancock Center in Chicago in 1970, which is one of the tallest buildings in the world. In the initial design stages, the Sears building went through a number of different design concepts, each one developed in an attempt to meet Sears's projected needs for the future.

Before talking with SOM, Sears thought 110,000 square-foot floors would work well for its buying and

Bruce Graham was the partner at Skidmore, Owings, and Merrill who was in charge of designing the tallest building in the world.

SKIDMORE, OWINGS, AND MERRILL

In 1936, partners Louis Skidmore and Nathaniel Alexander Owings opened what would become one of the world's largest architectural firms. Three years later, in 1939, John Ogden Merrill joined the firm that is today still called Skidmore, Owings, and Merrill (SOM). As the firm grew, they opened offices in San Francisco; New York City; Portland, Oregon; Washington, D.C.; and Chicago.

One of SOM's early projects was the designing of the town of Oak Ridge, Tennessee. It was there, during World War II, that the top-secret Manhattan Project developed the first atomic bomb. At the height of the project (1943–1949), 75,000 people lived in Oak Ridge. After the war, SOM turned toward the construction of large office buildings. Some of the notable buildings that came from SOM architects and that incorporated unique designs are: the Lever House (1952) in New York, the John Hancock Center (1970) in Chicago, One Shell Plaza (1971) in Houston, and the Sears Tower (1973) in downtown Chicago.

Designers from SOM have been both praised and criticized. Some praise their work for both the artful and sophisticated way in which they handle such big buildings. Others complain that designs for their buildings have a certain amount of "sameness" about them. Most, however, agree that the Sears Tower is SOM's most impressive building.

The original SOM team (left to right): Louis Skidmore, John Merrill, and Nathaniel Owings.

Partners from SOM also designed Chicago's John Hancock Center, which is one of the tallest buildings in the world.

merchandising departments. SOM designers and Cushman and Wakefield's marketing strategists, however, pointed out that it would be difficult to rent floors that were so large to other companies. Still, the first building proposal called for a 40-story building with 110,000 square feet per floor. This building was called the "Lump" by the design team. Soon it was agreed that the 110,000 square-foot floors would be a problem if Sears intended to rent out half of the building.

A number of proposals were discussed and rejected as the design team worked with the people from Sears. One trend was obvious: As the design evolved, the size of each floor decreased and the number of floors increased. Sixty floors of 70,000 square feet and 70 floors of 60,000 square feet were both rejected, as was a plan that called for two towers: a 60-story tower for Sears and a 40-story tower to rent out. As the design pushed upward and reached 104 stories, someone suggested that if they went 6 more floors, they would create the tallest building in the world. Such a building would also reach the 1,450-foot maximum height that the Federal Aviation Administration would allow them.

A Series of Tubes

Structural engineer Fazlur Khan had created a new system for building tall structures. He had discovered that a building constructed of a series of tubes, instead of a traditional steel skeleton, would be both lighter and stronger. For the John Hancock Center in Chicago, which proved the viability of the tube concept, Khan had included a number of diagonal supports that show on the outside of the building. These supports strengthen the tubular construction of the building by binding the tubes together, thus helping it stand up to the stresses of high winds. Khan and the rest of the design team convinced Sears that tube construction would make it possible to build the tallest building in the world without paying a premium for it. Khan, however, would have to come up with a new design solution to the wind problem if the Sears Tower was going to have its own unique look.

In the final design, the solution solved more than just the wind problem. The building starts out, at ground level, as a bundle of nine 75-by-75-foot steel tubes. This gives the lower-level floors just over 50,000 square feet of space. The nine tubes climb to the 50th floor intact, and then the first "setback" occurs. (A setback is when a building face is set some distance inside the wall of the building face just below it.) At this point, the tubes on the north-west and southeast corners end. The remaining seven tubes continue up to the 66th floor, where two of the remaining northeast and southwest corner tubes end. From the 67th floor to the 90th floor the four remaining tubes rise as a cruciform, a cross with equal arms. Above the 90th floor only two tubes remain, which means the uppermost 20 floors have only 12,283 square feet each.

The setbacks at the various levels work to dis-rupt the flow of air around the building, which reduces the force and eliminates the need for the diagonal bracing used in the Hancock building. The 75-foot tubes made the building weigh and cost less

FAZLUR KHAN: STRUCTURAL ENGINEER

Fazlur Khan devised the tube construction process for tall buildings.

Most people have heard of the country of Bangladesh because it is a place plagued by natural disasters and poverty. For Fazlur Khan—the structural engineer who is credited with creating the type of tubular construction that made the John Hancock Center and the Sears Tower in Chicago possible—Bangladesh was home. Interested in both physics and engineering, he attended the University of Dacca, in Dacca, Bangladesh, where he decided to concentrate on structural engineering. After graduating, Khan left his homeland to continue his studies at the University of Illinois, at Champaign-Urbana. After earning an advanced degree from the University of Illinois in 1955, he joined the firm of Skidmore, Owings, and Merrill (SOM) in its Chicago office.

When designing extremely tall buildings, a structural engineer has to contend with two natural forces: gravity and high winds. If constructed using traditional methods, extremely tall buildings would not be able to stand up to the pressures generated by these two forces. Khan is the person credited with coming up with a new way of building tall structures. Khan devised a system of tubes that are tied together in a structurally sound way. Not only is Khan's tube system stronger than traditional building methods, it is also cheaper. It has been estimated that the John Hancock Center would have needed an additional $15 million worth of steel had Khan's tube system not been used. The taller Sears Tower probably could not have been built any other way.

Computers have come to play a large part in the design and testing of structures, but as Khan has said, "Designs do not come from computers. They come from intuitive reasoning and are proved by computers."

than skyscrapers using traditional construction techniques. The steel used in the tubes weighs 33 pounds per square foot, while the steel used in conventional construction weighs an average of 50 pounds per square foot.

The varying floor sizes would make it easier for Cushman and Wakefield to find tenants for the upper floors, while the huge departments of Sears would occupy the 50,000-square-foot lower floors. In addition to solving practical problems, the setbacks create a more interesting shape than that of a plain rectangular building.

When first considered, the setback idea seemed to work in theory. The designers, however, needed practical proof before they suggested Sears spend the $160 million it would take to build the tallest building in the world. The designers sent two models of the Tower to the University of Western Ontario in London, Ontario, Canada, to be tested in the university's wind tunnel. The wind-tunnel tests proved Khan's theories about the setbacks, and the design now began to take its final form.

The Hidden Floors

There are floors designed into the Sears Tower that cannot be reached by the regular elevators. They were included for two reasons: First, they provide the space necessary to house the vast amount of equipment that heats, cools, and in other ways makes the building comfortable. Second, and more important, Khan saw a need to cross-brace his tubes. The cross-bracing occurs at floors 29–31, 31–33, 64–66, 88–90, 104–106, and 106–109.

Building Up
to the Sky

At a public ceremony on July 27, 1970, the completed design for the Sears Tower was shown to the people of Chicago. The mayor of the city, Richard J. Daley, thanked Sears "for the confidence they are showing in the future." The official Sears Tower ground-breaking ceremony took place shortly thereafter, in August.

The tallest building in the world would need a strong foundation. Some 180,000 cubic yards of

Opposite:
A welder works
on the Sears
Tower, high
above the city
of Chicago.

19

material were removed to make a 100-foot-deep hole. Two hundred watertight chambers, called "caissons," were built as a foundation for the building and the plaza that would surround it. Once the task of excavating and building the foundation was completed, the setting of the steel for the nine lower-level 75-by-75-foot tubes could begin.

By November 1970, the Tower's construction site had already been cleared.

The first 15-by-25-foot section of steel was set in place on June 7, 1971. The first nut was tightened by Gordon M. Metcalf, chairman of the board of Sears, and Arthur M. Wood, president of Sears. U.S. Steel Corporation made the steel for the building, and its construction subsidiary, American Bridge Division, was hired to erect the building. The steel was prefabricated into 15-by-25-foot sections called "Christmas trees" that could be both quickly and efficiently set and bolted into place.

By the end of the summer of 1971, the Tower had begun to rise and take shape.

The nine tubular units of the tower required 76,000 tons of steel, enough material to build more than 50,000 automobiles. The welding together of the Christmas trees was done using special equipment called "electroslag welders," which bind metal together using electricity rather than a flame. All the welds were then tested using ultrasonic testing equipment, and any flaws were repaired before the trees were shipped. All this prefabrication work saved a lot of time at the site.

Each tree consisted of a 25-foot-tall column with 15-foot-wide sections called "spandrels" attached to it. The location of the spandrels differed from tree to tree depending on where it was to be located in the tube.

Erecting the steel required special equipment that would be able to climb with the building. Set up inside the tubes were four 40-ton "creeper derricks,"—platformed cranes capable of lifting themselves up the inside of the steelwork as the building climbed.

The prefabricating of the Christmas trees by U.S. Steel made the erection of the tubes go rather quickly, and the Sears Tower rose at a rate of two floors per week. In a month's time, eight floors and more than 5,000 trees were added to the Tower. There were as many as 2,000 workers on the job at any one time, which also helped the construction work to progress rapidly.

Even though progress was being made quickly, the fact that this was to be the tallest building in the world did cause some unique problems for the

Opposite:
A great deal of construction work was done on the building's steel before it reached the site. Because of this, the structure rose quickly once the prefabricated materials arrived downtown.

After less than a year of actual construction, the Sears Tower was already many stories high.

builders. As the structure got taller, for instance, it became inconvenient and unpractical to get the workers down to the street for their meal breaks. To solve this problem, mobile catering kitchens were put on the 33rd and 66th floors.

As the Tower climbed, the wind—which had been a major concern for the designers—also began to cause problems, especially for the steelworkers. These workers were not afraid of heights and thought nothing of walking across a 6-inch-wide beam 1,300 feet above street level. At times, however, the wind blew so hard that the workers could not even stand up in it. The wind was the only thing that ever stopped construction work on the Sears Tower. By March 1972, the steel framework had reached the halfway point and was continuing upward at a regular rate. It would not be long before Chicago could boast a skyscraper that reached heights never before reached by human engineering.

Wind became a major problem for workers as the Tower rose. Many workers needed to scale ropes and narrow beams 1,000 feet in the air to do their jobs.

Topping Out

As the erection of the steel continued on the upper floors, the finish work began on the lower floors. Traditionally, large buildings were often faced with stone to make them look more like the classic structures that were built before steel became the building material of choice. The designers at SOM wanted the Sears Tower to look as modern as its design, and they wanted something that would be practical as well. Aluminum was chosen for the exterior face because of its efficiency, weight, and durability.

The Aluminum Skin

One problem with aluminum that the designers had to deal with was discoloration that the pollution and dirt of the city would cause.

Opposite:
By early 1973, the Tower had reached its final height and was nearly complete.

27

As a solution, the panels were anodized (a process in which an electrical current is run through the panels causing a coating material to fuse with the metal). The designers chose a coating that was dark enough to conceal the city's dirt.

After the anodized aluminum skin was in place, the workers could begin installing the Tower's 16,000 bronze-tinted windows. The floors where the cross-bracing and mechanical equipment

In 1972, work began on finishing the exterior of the Tower. A skin made of coated aluminum was chosen to cover the structure.

With the last beam hoisted in May 1973, only finishing work remained to be done.

were placed—the floors 29–31, 31–33, 64–66, 88–90, 104–106, and 106–109—received slotted covers to their openings rather than the bronze-tinted windows. The slotted floors can be seen easily and give the exterior of the building an even more distinctive look.

The Last Beam Rises

As the steel of the Tower stretched for the sky, the weather began to slow progress. From August to December 1972, the steelworkers were unable to work a full week. Studies of past weather conditions in Chicago had caused the construction companies to predict 8 lost days in December. By Christmas, however, they had already lost 11 work days in December. The temperature at 1,300 feet could be five to ten degrees colder than at street level, and the strong wind was always a problem.

Despite the challenges presented by the weather, on May 3, 1973, the last beam was hoisted to the top of the Tower. Mayor Richard Daley was present, along with 1,100 Sears employees and other people from the area, to watch the final beam travel the almost 1,500 feet from the street to the top of the building. A group of the Tower's electrical workers had formed a band, the "Tower Bums," and they performed a song that had been written for this locally televised occasion. The opening line of their song was, "She towers so high, just scraping the sky, she's the tallest rock."

The beam that was lifted into place on that day was unique. It had been on display at the side of the building for a period of time. People had been asked to sign it, and by the time it was lifted skyward, more than 12,000 construction workers, Sears employees, and other Chicagoans, including the mayor, had made their names a permanent part of the world's tallest building. The steelworkers had finished their part of the job, but there was still much to do before Sears and the other tenants could begin moving in.

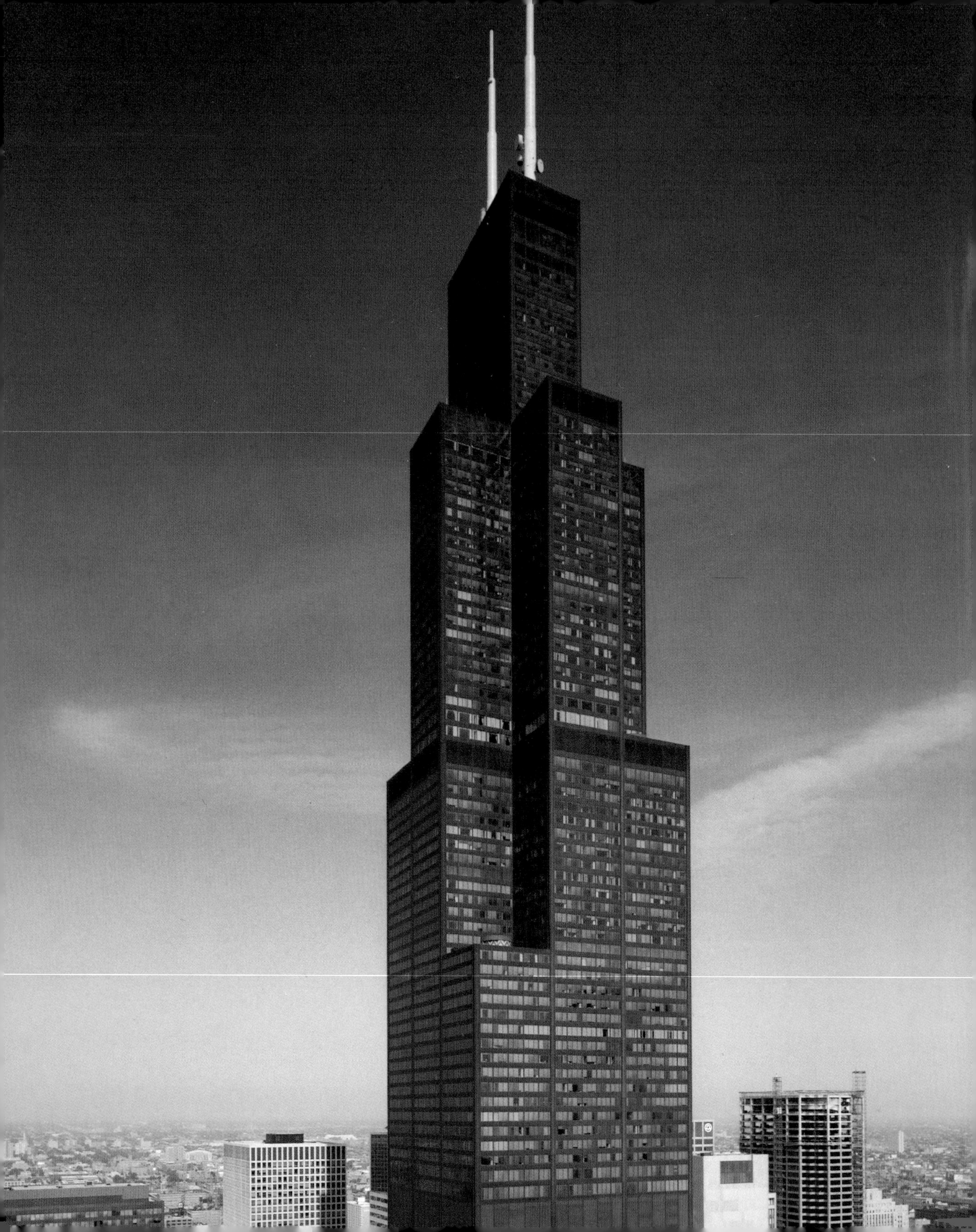

The Finishing Touches

As the floors were put in, the engineers planned another technique for dealing with the massive forces created by such a large building. The composite material used for the floors was laid in one direction for six floors and then in the opposite direction for the next six floors. This distributed the downward pressure of the building and helped to make the enormous structure more sound.

To be consistent with the modern look of the building, all the exterior and interior hardware,

Opposite: By September 1973, Sears workers began moving into the nearly finished tower.

33

which includes doors and the trim work in the lobby, was made of stainless steel. Inside the building, all of the public areas are covered with a special Italian marble. The outside plaza is done in red granite imported from Argentina.

By September 1973, the new Sears Tower was ready for people to begin moving in. This would be the sixth move for the leadership of Sears since the R. W. Watch Company left North Redwood, Minnesota, for Chicago in 1897. The last major move for the top management of the company had been in 1906, when it moved to its Chicago headquarters at Hoam Avenue and Arthington Street. People would be moving to the Tower from 13 different buildings at two locations in Chicago and one in Skokie, Illinois. On September 10, 1973, the first 400 employees moved into their new offices. Much of the moving—mostly of records and equipment— was done on the weekends, when it would be least disruptive to the employees.

At first, it looked as if the Sears Tower project would be a success. By 1974, eighty percent of the space that Sears would not be using was rented, and interest in the building from around the area was beginning to boom. The building itself, however, created a number of problems for its inhabitants.

The smaller, older buildings that Sears had been using had allowed workers to get to know one another and develop a sense of community within their workplace environments. The new building disrupted those communities and made the workplace cold and impersonal, especially for those workers on the huge 50,000-square-foot lower floors. Work hours

CALDER'S "UNIVERSE"

Inside the lobby of the Sears Tower is a 16,174-pound, 55-foot-wide, 33-foot-tall, metal sculpture that moves. The sculpture was commissioned by Sears and was created by Alexander Calder, one of America's best-known sculptors. The sculpture's movements are powered by seven different motors. The motors turn the many parts and the brightly painted elements of the work at different rates, creating the feeling of a moving "Universe." This is the title that Calder gave his work when it was unveiled on October 25, 1974. The metal parts of the piece were prefabricated in a foundry in Tours, France, under the direction of Calder himself. The pieces were then shipped to the Sears Tower, where they were assembled on site.

The son of two artists, Calder was born in 1898 and died in 1974. He started out as an engineering draftsman before becoming a sculptor. His

abstract sculptures are world famous, and many of them—like "Universe"—are made of metal, painted with bright colors, and capable of motion. Since the renovation of the lobby area was completed, "Universe" has become a much more appreciated part of the Sears Tower.

World-famous sculptor, Alexander Calder, created the sculpture that sits in the Tower's lobby.

had to be staggered to prevent people-jams at the doorways and lobby of the building and at the banks of elevators. Even with this staggering, employees had to plan to spend half an hour getting from the street to their offices each morning.

Because many employees on the larger floors never had an opportunity to look out a window during the day, Sears began announcing the weather at the end of the day so people would know what to expect when they left work.

It was true that the Sears Tower was state-of-the-art design and technology in action. But it seemed that Sears and the designers had failed to consider one important element enough: the people who worked inside. Once they were moved in, it became obvious to people that there was little "human" feeling in the offices. In fact, all this new technology only made most employees feel unhappy and disconnected from their jobs. Even some of the most modern conveniences of the new building were not appreciated by the Sears workers. Many people disliked the system of automated robots that delivered the mail. They felt it was just one more example of the unfriendly and "dehumanizing" nature of their new home.

In an attempt to address some of the problems that the employees were having with the building, Sears decided to renovate the lower public areas in 1982. The $20 to $30 million that was spent on the renovation opened up the lobbies and made it easier for both visitors and workers to get where they needed to be.

The biggest problem that the Sears Tower has faced since its opening in 1973, however, has not

During the 1980s and early 1990s, the future of the Sears Tower became uncertain.

been caused by the building. The decline of Sears as a leading force in the marketplace has affected the building and the company in the most serious way. Major competitors such as Wal-Mart, Kmart, and other discount retailers have cut deeply into Sears's business. When sales began to decline, Sears was so large that it could not react quickly enough to the changes in the marketplace.

In 1988, Sears put its Tower on the market for $1 billion. By June 1989, the company had four different bidders trying to buy the building. Olympia and York, a company from Toronto, Canada, offered Sears $1.04 billion for the Tower. The deal, however, fell through when the two parties could not agree on who would pay more than $200 million in property-transfer taxes. At that point, Sears decided to move to a new complex in the Chicago suburbs. Today, much of the Tower is empty, especially the huge, lower floors.

In 1990, after it was unable to come to terms with a buyer, Sears refinanced the mortgage on the Tower and received $815 million in the deal. The management of the building was then turned over to John Buck Company, a Chicago real estate developer. It was Buck's job to renovate the Tower and attract new tenants. Their first step was to hold a design competition among interior-design firms to come up with innovative ways to use the 50,000-square-foot lower floors. Buck also hired De Stefano and Partners to redesign the lobbies and other public areas. De Stefano knew the building well because he had been a partner at SOM before forming his own company.

An observation deck on the 100th floor of the Tower offers a unique view of downtown Chicago and its surroundings.

De Stefano was responsible for removing much of the "cold" interior elements and opening the spaces up to expose the interesting, structural aspects of Fazlur Khan's tubular construction. He also moved retail space to more practical areas. The much higher (50-foot-high) ceilings made the lobbies more appealing, and the Calder sculpture finally found a space that was equal to its impressiveness.

Buck also made progress filling the tower with tenants. Space that rented for $13 a square foot when the building opened was renting for as much as $33 a square foot on the higher floors. Despite the progress made, 1.5 million square feet of the Tower remained empty after the departure of Sears.

In November 1994, Sears Roebuck and Company officially announced that it was giving up ownership of the Sears Tower. During another refinancing, Sears officially transferred its ownership to the Boston-based firm of Aldrich, Eastman, and Waltch. Though Sears will no longer own the building, the new owners announced that the 110-story landmark would still be named the Sears Tower.

Visitors Keep Coming

Despite the problems faced by the owners in getting tenants for the tallest building in the world, tourists are drawn to the Tower at the rate of 1.5 million visitors a year. In redesigning the lobbies, De Stefano made sure that the tourists would not interfere with the people coming and going to their offices. Now there are special entrances for the sightseers and express elevators that send them rushing upward to the 100th floor sky lobby. A new visitor center has also been added with a variety of interesting displays about the history and skyline of the city below. A 185-seat theater was added to the visitor center, where a five-minute audiovisual show is presented to the visitors. The observatory is open every day of the year, and now many millions of people can claim they have been to the top of the tallest building in the world.

WASHING 16,000 WINDOWS AND MAINTAINING THE TOWER

Much of the Tower's exterior is glass.

Even the window-washing system for the Sears Tower is as modern as the design of the building. There are six automatic window-washing machines that are programmed to clean the entire exterior of the building eight times a year. These machines run on tracks on the outside of the building, and once the operator aligns the machine with the section to be cleaned, a button is pushed and the machine does the rest. The machine cleans 45 feet of the building per minute as it lowers itself down the tracks. The window washer sprays the building with water that has been mixed with detergent, brushes the windows and the aluminum skin of the building, and then vacuums up the water. The machines are so efficient that they filter and reuse the same water as they clean.

Much of the rest of the building is also automated. The Tower is all-electric, and a powerful computer monitors and controls the climate inside the structure as well as automatically shutting down the lights when the workday is finished. The 103 elevators are also controlled by the computer and are designed to get people to their floors as quickly and efficiently as possible.

The designers of the project also made provisions for dealing with the ice and snow that pile up in Chicago each winter. The sidewalks and plaza surrounding the Tower are heated to keep the ice and snow from accumulating on them. In the warm months, special street-sweeping machines keep the parking areas, sidewalks, and plaza clean.

As the world's tallest building, the Sears Tower offers a unique profile to the Chicago skyline.

GLOSSARY

aluminum An elemental metal that is both strong and lightweight.

anodize A process in which a coating is adhered to a metallic surface using electricity.

architect A person trained to design buildings and other structures.

caisson A watertight chamber used in the foundations of buildings built in wet areas.

Christmas tree A configuration of prebuilt steel components, as used in the construction of the Sears Tower.

crane A piece of construction equipment with a long arm for raising and lowering heavy materials such as steel beams and cables.

creeper derrick A specially designed crane that is able to climb up the structure that it is helping to build.

cross-bracing The structural crossing of metal beams to improve strength, as done in the joining of the six tubes of the Sears Tower.

cruciform Having the form or shape of a cross.

cubic yard The amount of material that it would take to fill a box three feet long on all sides.

electroslag welding A process in which pieces of metal are joined together using electricity to fuse them; additional metal is also used in the form of a welding rod.

granite A very hard and close-grained igneous rock, often used in buildings.

gross national product The total value of all goods and services produced in a country.

prefabricating Assembling parts of a building or other product before they are shipped to the site of their final assembly.

setback A building face that is set some distance inside the wall of the building face just below it. Due to the setback design of the Sears Tower, only two of the lowest-level nine structural tubes reach the 110th floor.

spandrels Horizontal and diagonal steel sections, as of the prefabricated "Christmas trees" used to build the Sears Tower.

structural engineer A person trained in the design of structures, the materials from which they are built, and the forces exerted by them.

suburbs The less densely populated areas that surround a city.

tubular construction The technique in which a building is constructed using a series of large self-contained units that are then bundled together. The Sears Tower starts out, at street level, as a bundle of nine 75-by-75-foot tubes.

ultrasonic analysis A technique in which high-frequency sound waves are used to analyze a substance, such as metal.

wind tunnel An enclosed space where high-powered, artificial winds can be generated to test the design of structures and other objects affected by the wind.

CHRONOLOGY

1886 Richard Warren Sears starts selling watches as a sideline to his job with the railroad.

1897 R. W. Watch Company moves to Chicago.

1964 John Hancock Center in Chicago is built, using a Skidmore, Owings, and Merrill (SOM) tubular design.

1969 Sears acquires the land for the Sears Tower.

1970 July 27—Design for the Sears Tower is made public.
August—Ground breaking for the Sears Tower takes place.

1971 June 7—First steel for the Sears Tower is erected.

1972 Tower's steel framework reaches halfway point.

1973 May 3—Tower's last steel beam is raised into place.

September 10—First 400 Sears employees move into the building.

1982 Public areas of the Tower receive their first renovation.

1988 Sears attempts to sell the Tower.

1990 Sears refinances the building for $815 million.

1993 Sears Tower public areas are renovated again, and efforts are made to improve space utilization to lease out more of the large lower floors, but 1.5 million square feet of the 4.5 million square feet remain vacant.

1994 Sears Roebuck and Company gives up ownership of the tower to a financial partnership managed by a Boston-based firm, Aldrich, Eastman, and Waltch.

FURTHER READING

Aylesworth, Thomas and Virginia. *Chicago*. Woodbridge, CT: Blackbirch Press, 1990.

Boring, Mel. *Incredible Constructions and the People Who Built Them*. New York: Walker & Co., 1985.

Davis, James E., and Hawke, Sharryl D. *Chicago*. Austin, TX: Raintree Steck-Vaughn, 1990.

Dunn, Andrew. *Skyscrapers*. New York: Thomson Learning, 1993.

Michael, Duncan. *How Skyscrapers Are Made*. New York: Facts On File, 1987.

Morgan, Sally and Morgan, Adrian. *Structures*. New York: Facts On File, 1993.

Source Notes

"All About Sears Tower." Sears Roebuck, 1974.

Barnhart, Bill, and Hodge, Sally Saville. "Original Cast Returning for Sears Tower Renovations." *Chicago Tribune*, November 14, 1983, section 3, 1.

"Cold Weather Slows Sears Construction." *Chicago Tribune*, January 7, 1983, section 12.

Enstad, Robert. "Girder Tops Sears 'Rock'." *Chicago Tribune*, May 4, 1973, 1.

"First Steel in Sears Building." *New York Times*, June 8, 1971.

Gapp, Paul. "Remembering the Gentle Giant Who Designed Sears Tower." *Chicago Tribune*, April 4, 1982, section 6, 28.

—"Sears Tower's Need for Changes Shows the Dangers of Thinking Too Big." *Chicago Tribune*, November 17, 1985, section 13, 14.

Haynes, V. Dion, and Wiltz, Theresa. "New Sears Site a Far, Better Place." *Chicago Tribune*, August 3, 1992, 1, 11.

Katz, Donald R. *The Big Store*. New York: Viking, 1987.

Kemla, Blair. "Towering Changes." *Chicago Tribune*, October 10, 1993, section 13, 20.

Kerch, Steve. "This Job Is a Tall Order." *Chicago Tribune*, October 20, 1991, section 16, 1.

Marlin, William. "Sears Tower." *Architectural Forum*, January 1974, v 140, 24-31.

"New Sears Building in Chicago Planned as the World's Tallest." *New York Times*, July 28, 1970, 18.

"A Not So Towering Sears Complex." *Chicago Tribune*, June 3, 1991, C-1.

Oppenheim, Carol. "Sears Begins Big Move to Tower This Weekend." *Chicago Tribune*, September 9, 1973, section 1.

Peterson, Bill. "Chicago Loses Bid for Sears." *Washington Post*, June 27, 1989.

"Planks Fall 108 Floors." *Chicago Tribune*, April 6, 1973, section 1.

Rodkin, Dennis. "Tower of Trouble." *Chicago*, v 43, February 1994, 50-55.

"Sears Tower Designers Tell Economics of Tube Design." *Chicago Tribune*, May 6, 1973.

"Sears Tower Skydeck Renovates." *Travel Weekly*, v 51, n 40, May 18, 1992.

Shuldiner, Herbert. "New Champ in the Skyscraper League." *Popular Science*, v 200, March 1972, 72-79.

"Skidmore, Owings, and Merrill." *Encyclopedia of Architecture*"

The Tallest Skyscraper." *Time*, June 11, 1973, 54..

Watley, Philip. "Sears Tower Ice Fall Spurs Panic Flight." *Chicago Tribune*, December 15, 1984, section 1.

Weil, Gordon L. *Sears Roebuck, USA: The Great American Catalog Store and How It Grew*. New York: Stein and Day, 1977.

"The World's Tallest: Saga of a Chicago Skyscraper." *New York Times*, October 18, 1970, section 8, 1, 7.

Yabush, Donald. "Victor Tower above All Other Steelworkers." *Chicago Tribune*, March 22, 1973, section 4A, 1.

INDEX